T0381225

The Intuitives Tool Belt

RONALD SCHAEFER

AuthorHouse™
1663 Liberty Drive
Bloomington, IN 47403
www.authorhouse.com
Phone: 1 (800) 839-8640

Published by AuthorHouse 01/30/2016

ISBN: 978-1-5049-7727-2 (sc)
ISBN: 978-1-5049-7728-9 (e)

Contents

A spiritual journey is not about reaching for something you do not have, but reclaiming what is already yours

CHAPTER 1

Imagination is Key

The first and foremost tool in your tool belt is your imagination. Now, I know what you are thinking: how is your imagination a tool? That is an easy question to answer. The imagination is your door way to the spiritual realm. Your imagination is what helps you get in touch with your guides, angels, and ascended masters, as well as different dimensions. As children, we all used our imaginations. I mean who has not played the floor is lava or had a tea party with dolls, stuffed animals, or even had an imaginary friend as a child? We have used our imagination all the times when we played by ourselves and with others, also when creating worlds in our minds as well as on paper, and when we paint or color pictures. That was the only way we knew how to interact with the world. However as we grew-up, we had been told that we had to leave that world behind. Sometimes we were told this by our peers, other times by our parents, and other times the situations in our lives made us grow up and leave that magical world behind. However in leaving that world behind, we left something ever precious there: our ability to connect to the subtle realm of spirit; to the infinite source of possibility. But you have nothing to fear because that realm is closer than you think and all we have to do is reacquaint ourselves with it. This is what the first chapter is going to be all about: tips and tools that you can use to open yourself back up to your imagination.

When I first started this journey myself, it was hard to connect with my imagination because my very dear friend TV had taken that away from me. How you ask? When you watch TV you go into the story that the writer creates for you and you are not really using your imagination, because you are letting someone else do it for you. So what I started to do was to limit how much TV that I watched, and believe me that was harder then it sounded because I had to occupy my time with other things. But what was I going to occupy my time with? What else was there to do that would distract me as long as TV would? So what I started to do was I started to walk. That was an amazing journey all in itself, by just going outside and enjoying nature. This gave me time to myself, which then lead me to see things in a different way and gave me time to really get to know myself at a deeper level. So the very first tool I want to give you to start your journey is to limit your TV viewing and get a hobby. It does not have to be walking. It can be whatever you want it to be such as coloring, painting, quilting, or blogging. Whatever is going to get you away from the TV will work.

The next tool is creative visualization. This is going to exercise your imagination muscles and it is also going to help you with manifesting, which is something we will talk about in a later chapter. Creative visualization is a very easy process first find a quiet spot be it in your home, the park or at work, just somewhere there is not going to be a lot of distractions. Now what I would like for you to do is to relax and to take 3 nice deep breaths into the nose filling the belly and then let it out slowly. Fill your belly three times with air and let it out. If you feel you need to release some tension on the 3rd and final breath let out the "AH" sound which will help in releasing tension from your body. Now what I would like for you to do is to close your eyes focus on your breathing and I want you to visualize a tree. It does not matter what kind of tree, just a tree and I want you just to hold that image in your mind. I want you to see how much detail you can see on the tree such as the design on the bark, does it have any moss on it, did you see branches and if so were there leaves on the branches and could you see how many. Now if you are having trouble seeing the tree or holding it for any amount of time, what you can do is get a piece of paper and you can write what you saw in vivid detail. Some people are very visual, while others are not and that is ok. These are just tools to help you awaken your imagination. This is not life or death and I do not want you to think of any of the tools I am giving you as that. If you cannot do any of them, then it doesn't mean that you have no imagination. Because that is not true at all, it simply means that you may have a different way of accessing your imagination. That is fine, because we are all different and we all have different strengths and weakness. Imagination and intuition or psychic energy are supposed to be fun and not put in a box, so please see all of these exercises as games you are playing and not life or death situations. The next tool is similar to daydreaming but also very different. Daydreaming is another great tool for not only awakening your imagination but also for manifestation. Now a lot of us day dream but most of the time it is unintentional. In this exercise we are making it intentional, so what I would like you to do is just to relax and breathe. I want you to just breathe and not think about what you have to do afterwards or what you are going to make for dinner. I just want you to relax and let your mind wander a little and if you need a suggestion because your mind is thinking of appointments, things you have to do or leading you to stressful or worrying thoughts, then what I would like you to daydream about is a safari. You are on safari in Africa and just let your mind linger on that or if that is a little too intense, then maybe you are on a cruise ship. Let your mind wander to where you are going and who are you with. It does not have to be for a long time, you can set a timer for 5 to 10 min to just let your mind wander into these fun possibilities.

Cloud watching is our next exercise. With cloud watching all you have to do is find a partly cloudy day and go outside and then just look at the clouds and wait to see what shapes you see in them such as a bunny or a sheep or a 3 headed dragon it does not matter just look and see. If you cannot see complex shapes like that then what shapes do you see? Do you see buildings or feathers? Do you see people or places? Just let your imagination run wild. Now by no means is your imagination limited to just seeing. You can incorporate or use any one or all of your senses when using your imagination. It just takes a little bit of practice and I am going to give you some tools to help you with that. The first is listening walks, a very simple technique that not only enhances your imagination but also your ability to mediate and tune in. As you go for a walk listen to all the sounds around you. As you hear the sounds, try to absorb them. Do not name the sounds; just listen without having any preconceived notions about them. Allow the sounds to flow through you; not just into your ears but your whole body and just let them flow in and out. Nature is a great place to do this, because the sounds are very soothing and not harsh at all. If you cannot or do not have access to a park, no problem just walk around your neighborhood.

The next exercise is about taste and we actually do this one more than we realize. Think about when you are told you are going to a restaurant, you imagine what the food is going to taste like based on your memory. You also do this when you look at pictures of food; you say that looks good and then you sometimes imagine how it might taste or smell. That is what I would like you to do now. Look at pictures of food you have tried and have not, and see if you can imagine how each would taste to you. Next exercise is to use your imagination for your sense of touch. Place different objects, things with different textures into a bag or box, and then what you do is stick your hand in there and see what feelings or sensations or even visions you get from the objects.

After reading the different ways to open up to your imagination, I bet you are asking yourself how any of these are really going to help me develop my intuition. What these exercises are actually doing; they are not only opening you up to your imagination, they are also opening you up to your "Clair abilities." Now what are Clair abilities?? First let's look at the word Clair, which is a French word that means clear. Now your Clair senses are tied to your five senses. They are just the senses that pick up on the more subtle energy of the world. Everyone has them and some Clair abilities may be stronger in others. For example for me it is my clairvoyance and Clair cognition that are stronger, so for me I clearly see and clearly know. But just like there are 6 senses, there are also 6 Clair.

1. ***Clairvoyance*: Is the ability to see. It is not just the ability to see the future but also the past as well as aura and other dimensions.**

2. ***Clairaudience:* Is the ability to hear spirits and other dimensional beings such as angels and guides, as well as being able to hear about past present and future events, hearing what has happened or might happen.**

3. ***Clairsentience* is the ability to get information by feeling with your whole body**

4. ***Clairscentsi:* the ability to smell fragrances odors, or substances which are not in your surroundings.**

5. ***Clairsentience* the ability to taste a substance without putting it in our mouth.**

6. ***Clair cognition*: The ability to clearly knowing without any external influence.**

All of these are great and interesting abilities and each has their positive and negative sides, but you have each one inside of you. One may be stronger than the rest, just like with hobbies you may be a great baseball player but you are terrible at soccer. We all have strengths and weakness. You may be asking yourself: well how do I know which one is my strongest? The easiest way to figure that out is with a very easy tool. When you first meet someone what are you most drawn to? The way they look, the way they make you feel, or do they seem interesting to you. You may be drawn to the way their voice makes you feel or the way they smell, or what taste you get in your mouth when they come around. Each of these represents one of your Clair senses. If you are first drawn to the way they look, then your strongest Clair ability is most likely clairvoyance which means you clearly see. If you are drawn to how interesting they are or you just want to know more about this person, then maybe Clair cognition which means that you clearly know is one of your strongest abilities. If you are drawn to how they make you feel, then you are most likely a clairsentience, which means that you clearly feel. If you are drawn to the way that they smell or the odor that comes from them without the aid of perfume, then you are most likely a clairscent which means you can clearly smell. If you are drawn to the taste you get in your month when this person enters the room you are most likely a clairgustance which means that you clearly taste. Now if you are like me and you find yourself able to tap into one or more of these abilities, then you may be a spiritual intuitive which means that you can tap into any one of the Clairs at any time. Just realize that while you may only be strong with one or a couple of abilities, that you are still able to work on and develop the others. In the meantime others may be able to do the same just not with the same ease that you might have with it and vice versa.

Let's move on now into some psychic development exercises that helped me when I was developing my intuitive skills. However, before we go into any more exercises, what I want to express to you is that these exercises are not the end all be all. If you cannot do one, that it is ok or if you just don't feel a resonance with one of the exercises, it is not a problem. Each person is different and one may work better for you than another, and another person may just skip it and that is fine. The one thing that I want to make very clear is that psychic energy is fun and cannot be kept in a box. If you try to contain it, control it, make it fit into what you expect it to be, then you are losing out on great growth. When doing these exercises just let things happen, so you may learn and grow.

Personally I tried a card exercise which is what I am going to share with you now. When I first started this new exercise; wow I was terrible and it was discouraging. I would literally only get maybe 1 or 2 correct and then I would feel frustrated and say that I am not intuitive and just give up. But then some time later something would happen when I would know what was going to happen before it did, or I would see a vision of something and then it would come true. All of these things have continually brought me back to these exercises. It wasn't until 2011, that I finally got serious and I decided to just stick with it. After only 4 weeks I was getting to be really good and I was getting more right than I was wrong. I would still have my moments where I would get like seven in a row right and then get one wrong and then the next and the next but instead of letting that stop me, I took this as an opportunity to stop and breathe and re-center myself and just try again. Sometimes if I was still not feeling the flow you know what I did, I just stopped and walked away and would try again another time. Now look at me, I am writing a book on how to do this. So be gentle with yourself and see how far you can go and give yourself as well as your spirit time. This is just like any other skill; you do have to work at it. You do not expect that a skier got that good overnight or Michael Jordon was just that amazing. No, they practiced and that is what you have to do is to practice and it is ok to take a day or two off as long as you get back on the wagon. Now let's move on to the actual exercises. The first one is the one I mentioned above. For this exercises all you need is a deck of playing cards. Make sure they are just the red and black ones, no other colors for right now. What I want you to do is to just take three nice big deep breaths and calm your mind, clear out any expectation of the outcome, and become as clear minded as you can. Now what I want you to do is to pick up the first card and do not turn it over. Just pick it up and you are going to try to tell what color the card is. It was helpful to me to close my eyes and ask what color is this card, but this may not work for you which is ok if it doesn't. Another way you could try is to close your eyes and rub the card in between your hands. I would like you to see if you can sense the color of the card if it is black or red and not the numbers etc. The reason I would like for you to work with the colors first is because it is simpler and getting you used to the concept and idea of frequency and vibration for the colors. Each color in the world has its very own vibration or frequency to it. Red and black are the easiest colors because they have the longest wave lengths, but if you would like to start with shapes, that will also be fine. This is your journey; I am just a guide on your journey. Once you have mastered that then you can move on to what shape is on the card and then you can branch out to Uno cards and see if you can pick up the different colors on these cards. Another exercise that you can try is the Zener cards and you can find those online if you think you are going to do better with shapes and you do the same thing that you did with the playing cards except you are doing it with shapes. I recommend that you back the Zener cards with something so you cannot see threw them. The last exercise I would like to share with you in this chapter is a two in one exercise with how to help you start to see auras. The first and the easiest way is to have you stand in front of a mirror and against a white wall. Now let your eyes relax, breathe and just stare at the side of your head and just let your vision soften a little and what will start to happen is a white film will begin to form, do not try and look at it just keep your eyes on the spot you are staring at and what will start to happen is the white film will start to have a color. What you are doing is, you are starting to tune into the aura and as you practice you will become better at it and you will not have to stare so long. Another exercise to start seeing auras is to get a piece of poster board white and drawn a spiral on it try to make sure all the lines are as equal distant as you can then once again center yourself take some nice deep breaths and stare at the center of the spiral you just drew with that soft gaze even if it starts to fade out keep that soft gaze do this every day for about 5 to 10 minutes and this will also start to help you see auras. Finally the last exercise which goes along with the spiral exercises is to take 3 by 5 note cards and trace a triangle, square, and circle on them, then shade in the white parts around it so you only have the white in the middle of the shape. Now what you do is with only your eyes start going around the outline of that shape and what this is going to do, is to strengthen the cones and rods in your eye making it easier to pick up the more subtle frequencies of light. This is going to be an amazing journey and I am excited and honored to be on it with you. I just want you to remember that becoming intuitive or psychic is fun but it also has difficult times. Make sure when doing any of these exercises to always have an element of light heartedness too, because if you take it too seriously then you put yourself in a box and cannot grow to make any headway in the direction that spirit would like you to go. I am sending you all my love and support.

CHAPTER 2

The Ego: Enemy or Ally?

What is the ego, before we begin to see if it is our ally or our enemy? The ego is your self-esteem; the way you feel about yourself and it is also the part of your brain that goes between the conscious and the unconscious which meditates reality. The ego is also the part of the brain that wants to keep you safe. That is its job to make you alert, and to be aware of any threats to you. This aspect of the ego comes from your ancestors in ancient times when they always had to be on alert to be aware of danger at any time. That is what the ego is; but what does it really do for us? Does it really need to be there or is it just a bygone of the past? What the ego does is it takes all of our unconscious beliefs and brings them to the conscious mind. When we are given a choice of something or when making a decision on something the ego comes into play. Let's take for example when you were younger you went to the pool with your parents it was a great time, except when you slipped and almost drowned. your ego then takes that experience and sees it as an attack or a time when your physical life was endanger, so it then creates a boundary or a fear about the pool so that so it can help you sustain your physical life. So now you may not like the pool or you may have a fear that it will happen again, your ego made the belief subconsciously and now it is a fear. Now did the ego do this on purpose? No, it was following its main programming, which is to protect you by physically keeping you safe and alive. Because the ego automatically does this and sometimes during the process prevents us from doing things we would really like to do because of these fears it created to keep us safe, many people may view the ego as an enemy. But really the ego is just following programming and the great thing is that you can reprogram it. So now that we have talked about what the ego is, let's talk about what it can do for you and how you can shift yourself from saying your ego is bad or your enemy, to your ally. We now know that the ego takes your beliefs and in turn brings them to the conscious. So what can we do with that information? What we can do now, is to go through the ego to see what your beliefs are and then either alter these beliefs or delete them all together and replace them with a new belief that will better serve you now. How to do this is easy, if you are willing to do the work. What I did was, I went into meditation because I wanted to see my core beliefs, the beliefs that make me who I am. Once I did, then I was able to see those core beliefs, the ones that support me and then change the ones that did not. It has taken work to change these beliefs. Do not think for one minute just because you find them and say ok let's change, that you are done. It is not quite that easy. You have to write down your new beliefs and then after that you have to review them, until they become you're your new beliefs. There is a tool I like to use that really helped me. Personally I *had* a hard time with money and making ends meet, so I would say out loud "NO that's not me anymore, I am grateful that I have all the money I need to pay all my bills and have $100 left over." I would say it and then move on and if thus worrisome thoughts would come back, I would just say it again and again because in doing this repeatedly I am training my ego that this is my new belief about my financial situation. Once it became my new belief guess what happened, I now have all the money I need to pay all my bills and buy groceries and still have $100 dollars left over because that is my new mind set. The nice thing is that once you change your beliefs, you change your reality. When trying to tune into your intuition, we often run into the problem of the ego overriding the voice of your intuition. This is another reason that people perceive the ego to be an enemy, but remember the ego is doing its job. At some point you either told yourself or were told to not listen to your gut feelings or your intuition, because it was silly, or you just shrugged it off whenever you had those feelings. By doing this you essentially told your ego that your belief is that we are not going to listen to those feelings hence your intuition, which is why people say all the time that they are not intuitive or that they are not connected to their intuition or psychic abilities. A tool that I found that had worked for me was making an ego contract. Which is basically making a legal document with yourself and your ego understands law so if you sign a contract that you are obligated to follow the terms of it. Basically what you are doing is bypassing the egos defensive mechanisms so that you can start to listen to your intuition more and your ego less. Below is an outline if you would like to use it you can always make up your own.

I, (insert your name,) the party of the first hereby thank you Ego for doing your job.

1. *Keeping me safe*
2. *Abiding by the beliefs I hold*
3. *Keeping track of the beliefs I hold*
4. *Helping me make safe choices based on past experiences*
5. **However, I no longer wish you to be the only guiding force in my life I now wish to listen to the voice of my intuition. Ego by signing and entering into this contract which is legally binding you are no longer aloud to.**

__Interrupt me in meditation with thoughts of the day__
__You are not aloud to interject when I am asking my spiritual team__(I.E guides angels masters and past over loved ones)
__You are not allowed to put your input in to my spiritual matters at this time.__
__When I attempt a psychic exercise you can not interject unless asked to.__
Ego you the second party understand this and by signing this you hereby agree to all the terms and conditions of this document.

X _____ date _____

X _____ date _____

This is your ego contract you are more than welcome to change it in any way to make it so your ego understands that you are going to be listening to it less and your intuition more. This is just like an affirmation, read it a couple of times and then you have to listen to the voice of your intuition. The voice of the intuition is different from the voice of the ego. The voice of the ego is loud and makes you feel tight or afraid, while the voice of your intuition is co*mpletely* different. The voice of your intuition is soft like the beat of butterflies wings it will make you feel good and relaxed and will come very naturally. I will not lie to you and tell you once you do this that your ego will stop, no it will not. It is a part of you and it will fight back and try to keep you under its control to protect you. The ego will get in the way and be annoying, but this is a part of the process and within two months or so as you tune in to your intuition more and your ego less you will see a difference.

CHAPTER 3

The Energy within Awakens
(Your energy centers)

There are energy centers that exist within the physical body that are archetypes for different thought patterns and these are known as your chakras. Within us exist seven main chakra points which allow both physical and etheric energies to flow through us, and there are also six to seven more outside of the physical body but right now we are only going to be talking about the seven within the body. The chakras each have a different color which corresponds with their energy wavelengths as well as a sound; the first one that we are going to start with is the root chakra.

Root/base chakra: color corresponding is blood red
Sound on the musical scale in which it is associated with is: Do
Other sound it is associated with is: Lam
Element that is associated with is: Earth
Relates to part of the body: adrenal glands
Keyword: "I have"

Sacral chakra: associated with the color orange
Sound on the musical scale: Ray

Other sound it is associated with is: Vam
Element that is associated with is: water
Relates to part of the body: genitals
Keyword: "I want"

Solar plexus chakra associated with the color: yellow
Sound on the musical scale: Me
Other sound it is associated with is: Ram
Element associated with is: fire
Relates to part of the body: pancreas, adrenal glands
Keyword: "I can"

Heart chakra associated with the color: emerald green
Sound on the musical scale:Fa
other sound:Yam
element associated is: air
relates to: Thymus
keyword:" I love"

Throat color associated with: blue/sky-blue
sound on the musical scale:So
other sound:Ham
element associated with: sound
relates to: thyroid
keyword:" I speak"

Third I color associated with: indigo
sound on the musical scale:La

other sounds:OM
element associated with is: light
relates to: pituitary gland
keyword:" I see"

Crown color associated with is: Violet/purple
sound on the musical scale:Te
other sounds:OM
relates to: penile gland
keyword:" I know"

These are the seven chakras but this is a very basic knowledge on them I want to go ahead and expand on each of them, however before I dive in I do want to say that your chakras can be blocked. Later I will get into some symptoms of how you know your chakras are blocked and some ways that you can unblock them, but there is one sure fire quick way to do this, and the quickest way to realign and clear your chakras is to simply saying the musical scale Do, Ra, Me, Fa, So, La, Te, Do the sound that you make when singing these notes move through your body and can help to open up your chakras or perhaps realign them which ever you need help with. I would also like to state that the chakra system is not permanent it is not something that you will continuously work with it is something that when you are starting out will help you to attune and recognize different energies but once you become accustomed to the more subtle energies if you choose you can get rid of your chakra system it will not harm you or hurt you and it will only be done once your higher self (which we will talk about in another chapter) allows that to happen and you will know when but for now let us stick with the energy system right now. Let's jump right in to the first chakra which is the root/base chakra this chakra is related to survival and the physical body as well as money, safety, and shelter is located at the base of the spine this chakra is used for grounding yourself a great way to see or to energize this chakra is to see a red anchor coming out of the base of your spine and going deep into the earth. Some ways you can see if there is a blockage within this chakra is by your body being constipated or fatigued or emotionally there may be a blockage if you feel spacey or ungrounded or unsafe. A great way to clean and clear or even activate this chakra is to wear the color red or even have a red post it note in your pocket you could also do a meditation to find out what is blocking that chakra and use the Violet flame to help transmute whatever lock or fear is there. This may sound strange but you can also sit underneath the tree and asked the spirit of the tree to help ground you you could imagine its roots helping you to ground yourself deep within the earth. The next chakra is the Sacral chakra is located two finger lengths below your belly button it relates to the emotions and desires, creativity, sexuality this chakra is where your creative juices come from as well as your sex drive. Wasted no it is blocked in the physical body is you may experience painful periods lack of sex drive low testosterone or estrogen emotionally you may have a low sex drive or creative blocks. For this chakra you can once again wear the color that is associated with it also to find out what the blockage is of course doing it a meditation to help you find out what the blockage or fear may be. A way to activate this chakra is to go out in nature or you may also go to a museum and look at all the beautiful paintings or of course as I said before go out in nature and look at all the beauty around you, you can also go out and get yourself what I like to call an emotional notebook, this is where you can start writing down how you feel even if you feel nothing why? What does that feel like physically, emotionally, spiritually, and mentally once you begin to express how you feel more emotions will come and of course something else you can do is to have a good cry or laugh that's always healthy. I remember when I was first working on unblocking one of my chakras I actually laughed so hard that I cried which is what I needed the laughter was just a gateway for me to feel safe to express how I was really feeling at that time. The next chakra is the solar plexus also known as the naval chakra is located two finger length above the bellybutton it's related to desires, self-control, self-esteem as well as Claire senti and meaning to clearly feel through the whole body. This chakra is all about personal power you know when this is blocked in the physical body by poor digestion and or low blood sugar you can know that this chakra is blocked within your emotions by low self-esteem or lack of willpower you let people walk all over you. With the other chakras you can of course wear the color yellow or meditate on it to see what the blockage is. This was the toughest chakra for me to open and to clear because of many different reasons one reason was because of my childhood in school let's just say I was not the most popular person nor did I believe in myself I cared so much what other people thought of me I did not think anything of myself I let others opinions decide who I was going to be. It also came for a past life issue as well however I have now unblocked that chakra and with the help of Archangel Chamel who is associated with this chakra as well as the unicorns I have now opened this chakra fully and hence why I am writing this book now. The next chakra is the heart center which is located in the center of the chest is related to love and forgiveness compassion and self-love. You know when this chakra is blocked physically when you experience some of these symptoms heart problems such as heart attack stroke which are the most extreme also high cholesterol may be another sign that your heart chakra is blocked. Emotionally you know the chakra is blocked when you enter a bout of depression or feeling no enthusiasm for life a general lack of motivation. One of the best ways to unlock your heart chakra is to have a good laugh it helps to release any pent up frustrations or emotions that you have inside of course just as the other chakras you can wear the color that is associated with it or meditate on the blockage another great way is to hug a spruce tree if there is not one readily available hugging any tree will do and if there are no trees around then you can always hug a person or a pet and not just a quick side hug a real hug is what you need to open the chakra. The next chakra is the throat which is also connected to the ear chakras and to declare audience ability which means to clearly hear this chakra is located in the middle of the throat where the Adams Apple lies. This chakra is blocked physically if you lose your voice or have trouble such as strep throat or a permanent sore throat you may also experience in her ear problems many ear infections may plague you you may also experience thyroid problems such as hypothyroidism or hyperthyroidism this chakra deals with speaking your personal truth and communication you know when this chakra is blocked emotionally when you are unable to speak your truth you can unblock this chakra by once again wearing the color that is associated with it meditating on the block or by singing or writing down your truth. The next chakra is the third eye chakra which is located in between your eyebrows this chakra is associated with clairvoyance which means to clearly see this can mean that you clearly see past, present, or future events that have yet to happen you may also experience prophetic dreams or visions. Ways to know that this is blocked within the physical body you experience sinus pressure ways to know what is blocked emotionally is you have a lack of vision for the future a lack of direction ways to unblock this chakra are two of course wear the color that is associated with it also just to meditate meditation is the gateway to this chakra. The last chakra is the crown chakra is located at the very top or crown of the head is associated with universal knowledge also the ability of clear cognizance which means to clearly know you know this chakra is blocked physically when you experience migraines or headaches that lasted more than two days you know this chakra is blocked emotionally when you feel alone uninspired lack of love lack of creativity lack of inspiration you can unblock this chakra by wearing the color that is associated with it and just like the third eye chakra meditating on it and beginning to explore the metaphysical or paranormal realm when your crown chakra is blocked what it means is that you are ready to experience more you no longer are occupied by the mundane you know that there is more out there and you wish to explore it. There is another way to help clean and clear all of your chakras you can of course call on the archangels that are associated with each of the chakras within meditation or sleep a great affirmation which is what we are going to talk about in the next chapter to use for this either when going to sleep or awake is dearest angels I ask that you work with me in my sleep tonight to help clear away any blocks that are keeping me from fully enjoying my life please either call these blocks to my attention or completely removed them from my mind and body during sleep tonight thank you with gratitude.

Archangels:

Uriel: crown

Raziel/Rafael: third eye

Gabriel: throat

Chamel/Rafael: heart(both can be used for this chakra for the chakra is not purely emerald green since it is associated with love you may also use shim you well and pink light personally I like to use both angels)

Chamuel: solar plexus

Ariel:Sacral

Michael: base/route

you can of course go online and look up crystals/stones that are also associated with these chakras there vibration and energy will help to open and clear or strengthen the chakra it is associated with.

CHAPTER 4

Psychic Protection

As you being to open up to the wonderful world of spirit it's time to talk about psychic protection. I am not going to tell you that there is nothing negative out there or entities that are not trying to trick you, because they are out there however you will not run into them unless your vibration calls them and it's all about vibration when it comes to entities you only attract to you what your vibration is. I attribute me not running in to many because of the psychic protection I have put up, there are many different ways to protect yourself in this chapter we will be going over those ways in which to protect yourself. The first way that I ever heard of to protect yourself which shielding your self with white light and boy let me tell you did that work, however something that I noticed was that it cut me off from everything else when you surround yourself with the white light from head to toe completely surrounding yourself is a great protection mechanism, however what the white light does is it completely blocks you off from anything coming in or anything getting out. So let us say that you are in a situation where you are feeling extremely anxious you then surround yourself with the divine white light of God, what then what happens is you are trapping that anxious energy inside with you. Instead of surrounding yourself with white light what I like to do is surround myself with pink light and say that it is porous and that I only allow unconditional love or higher in so that way if I am in the situation where I am feeling anxious then the energy is able to escape and I am able to call in a more calming and peaceful energy. Another great way to begin to protect yourself psychically is by making boundaries for yourself what I like to do is put my hands out in front of me fully extended your arms out and imagine as your arms extended out in either direction that you are forming an energetic pink wall go around your self four times making each wall then put your hands above you make a wall and then put your hands below you and make a wall what you can say as you are doing this is no negative or outworn energies entities or belief systems may enter minefield I am a being of unconditional love and only unconditional love or higher may enter. What this is going to do is one you have set an intention saying that you are being of love and you only wish to experience love so that is what you will bring to you the second thing that you are doing is you are creating that field around you now anyone in a lower vibration will be unable to come within your field without either raising to your vibration or only able to stay with you for a short period of time before they have to get away from you because there vibration is not raising to where yours is so they are unable to stay within your presence. You also have a built in protection mechanism is your guardian angel everyone is born with a guardian angel you are actually born with two you have an introverted guardian angel who is always at your back always gently stroking your auric field clearing you as best as possible and calming you then you have your extroverted guardian angel your extroverted guardian angel is your protector is the one who pushes you out of harms way gives you intuitive hints such as a feeling to turn left instead of right or a whisper of your name so you don't cross the street at the wrong time. What these two beings do is they both protect you but on different levels you're more introverted angel protects you on a spiritual level also this angel brings to you, peace and reassurance. Your extroverted guardian angel is the one who protects you within the physical world and make sure that you do not die before you have decided to or have contracted into this angel is the one that you can call on to protect you within the 3-D. I had a wonderful experience with my guardian angel what had happened was my boss at work was always coming in and being very negative always bringing me down telling me different things that I needed to fix on a daily basis and wants one thing was fixed it was never good enough I was had to redo it or someone else would have to come in and do it for me this became very degrading and it made me really hate work, so what I did was I asked my guardian angel to please stand at the door and to not allow any negative energies into the room and I envisioned my guardian angel standing at the doorway and what do you know, my boss past my room all day and never came in once which was amazing since she came in every day. I wanted to see how long this would last so what I did was once again I placed my guardian angel at the door and said guardian angel please don't allow any negative energy into this room and once again envisioned him there but this time to save time I asked him whenever I came into work to stand at the door and not allow any negative energy in that whole week my boss past my door and if she did come in it was for a brief minute or so and she said nothing negative merely told me what my break schedule was for that day, I tried it again the next week and it still worked I was absolutely amazed by this and thanked my guardian angel daily for all the protection that he had given to me and I still use this technique to this day even though that boss is now gone. Why is psychic protection so important? Why do we need to protect ourselves, without proper protection we are open to anything and anyone and you don't want to live in everyone else's skin, emotions, or mental clutter. When you become open to spirit you become open to the wide range of energy that is within our world and as you begin to open up more and more you become more sensitive to the energies around you that is why it is essential for you to have a form of psychic protection. Without the aid of psychic protection you would take on all the things in the world you would take on all your friends coworkers or families negative emotions that would then bring you down which would then bring your down your vibration and then you would draw in more negative experiences. A lot of people ask me how I get to know my guides how will I know it's my guide I want to make sure that I am only communicating with my guides a great technique that I used that I learned from the wonderful psychic intuitive Diana Hall, was to ask for guidance and protection during any of my readings first of all the second thing that I learned was a great technique to ensure that you only talk to and receive guidance from your highest guides and angels.

The first step to this is to sit in a comfortable position and begin to breathe deeply in through the nose filling up the diaphragm and breathing calmly and slowly I like to keep a rhythm of three seconds breathing in through the nose filling the diaphragm then holding it for three seconds and then releasing that breath through the mouth for three seconds this it's you into a pattern this gets your body too, down as well as your mind the first thing that you would want to do is imagine roots either coming from your root chakra all the way down to the core of the earth. Then what I would like for you to imagine is a beautiful cylinder or two of light coming down around your whole body this is you were golden white light then I would like for you to imagine your body made of you were light I would like for you to see your self going up in this tube of light I would like for you to see the sun and to fill your self with the sun's energy with love with light and protection and wisdom imagine the sun filling you with its light and combining with your light body now I would like for you to imagine yourself going over to the moon and asking the moon for the same energy for love, light, protection and imagine the energy of the moon which is silver in touring into your light body then where I would like for you to imagine is your light body ascending higher and higher up in two a portal this portal will take you to where your soul came from back to source you may see many different things through the portal you may see lights you may see images or you may just feel as if you are moving even though you have not moved physically at all once you reach your final destination asked the universe/God/source to please fill you with love, light, protection and wisdom for the divine highest good of all see your self being infused with that energy from source. Then what I would like for you to do is imagine yourself traveling back down that two of light and reentering your physical body with the tube of light still surrounding you then I would like for you to imagine either from your root chakra which is located at the base of the spine or from the soles of your feet roots going deep down into the earth all the way to its molten core then what you can do is you can call in Archangel Michael and ask him to surround you with the circle of angels as well is a circle of angels around your house or just around your room or just placing them in front of you behind you and to the left side of you or to the right side of you or you may also choose just to put an angel at the window and an angel at the doors of your room it is all up to you. Then you may ask to be attuned as well as invoke your highest guides and angels to come with in your order field you must always invite your highest guides and angels and they cannot come to you unless they are invited because that would be a breach of free will that only happens in times when you are in great danger or when you may be killed and you are not supposed to die at that particular moment. After you attune yourself to your highest guides and angels you can then attune your self and invoke the archangels the archangels I like to invoke and attuned to are as follows; Archangel Michael, Archangel Raphael, Archangel Gabriel, Archangel Uriel, Archangel Metatron, Archangel sandaphone, Archangel Raziel then I like to call in all other archangels who wish to be present at this time who wish to work with me for my divine highest good, lastly you can call in all energies and entities and emissaries of light within the universe who wish to work with you at this time for your divine highest good. The final step to this is to attune your heart to the highest most unconditional loving energy in you and in the universe at this time after doing all of this you just sit in meditation and you can allow whatever information your highest guides and angels as well as the archangels or emissaries of light have for you. I know that may seem very lengthy however it is a great protection tool and not only is a great protection it also allows you to only attune to what is going to serve you in the highest good. When you first try this technique know that you may have to open your eyes and reread what I have written or you can come up with your own way of doing this whatever works for you. Another great protection tool is to call in Archangel Michael asked Archangel Michael to surround you with the circle of angels ask him to surround your home or dwelling with the circle of angels then ask God to send down his divine golden white light and clear out all negative and outworn energies, entities, belief systems that no longer possibly serve, then you can ask Archangel Michael to please use his sword of truth to let you only speak with those beings who have your highest good in mind. I have mentioned a couple of different psychic protection techniques but this is by no means an exhaustive list these are just some of the ones that I have use if they do not resonate with you if you do not think that they will work for you that is totally fine what I would like for you to do is maybe play around with them combine them together see what works for you because we have to remember psychic energy cannot be put into a box psychic energy must be free. There is one more type of psychic protection that you can use it is more physical than any of the others all the rest of these are within the imagination this however is within the physical world you can use stone there are specific stones that are good for psychic protection here is a list of just some of the stones agate, alum, amber (used extensively by Ancient Romans), apache tears, aventurine, banded agate, beryl, black agate, black kyanite, black obsidian, calcite, carnelian, cat's eye, chalcedony, chrysoprase, citrine, chiastolite, coral, dravite, eisenkiesel quartz,emerald, fire agate, flint, fluorite, fossils, gold, golden topaz, halite (rock salt crystal), heliodor (golden beryl), hematite, herkimer diamond, holey stones, honey calcite, imperial topaz, jade, jasper, jet, labradorite, lapis (lapis lazuli), lava, lepidolite, magnesite (lodestone), mahogany obsidian, malachite, marble, mookaite, moonstone, nuumite, ocean jasper, olivine, pearl, peridot, petrified wood, prehnite, pumice, pyrite, quartz, quartz crystal clusters, now by no means is this an exhaustive list there are plenty of other stones that you can look up on the Internet just by doing a simple Google search for psychic protection crystals/stones.

CHAPTER 5

Intent not content

We all have heard the saying read between the lines. But what does that really mean? Well as an intuitive or psychic we do this all the time. When someone says oh I am fine, we can pick up that they are not fine. The content of what they said and the intention behind it was not the same. If we just listen with our ears, we will only hear the content of words, it is not until we start listening with our hearts, that we can truly hear what others are saying. As we discussed in the previous chapter the heart chakra is located in the middle of the chest and it is associated with the keyword "I love." So how is the heart going to listen? How can you actually hear what people are saying with your heart, when your heart does not have ears? Your heart may not have ears, but your heart does have an electromagnetic field that is 10 times larger than the one around your head and that is how your heart is able to hear. It takes the vibrational frequency of what people are saying and then translates it and hears the truth and the real intention of what people are saying to you. I remember when I first tried listening with my heart and what I had done was of course took a big deep breath and then I put my hands over my heart and I set the intention to hear with my heart all that day. Later that day we went to go look at a house that we were thinking about renting and when we arrived there were two other groups there as well. One group was a family and the other group just seemed to be roommates. So we all greeted each other and everyone was very nice, then we all went inside and began looking around the house.

The roommate couple did not like the style of the house and they left. So then it was just me and my mom along with the other couple who had a child. Their child was running everywhere very excited while the mother and father seemed very reserved. All of us came downstairs into the kitchen where we met with the realtor and she proceeded to tell us the different perks of the house and how much the rent was. My mom and I were not going to get the house because it was out of our price range, but we said thank you and we would think about it. The other couple stayed and they were still talking to the realtor. We said goodbye and as we did the wife said have a good day and goodbye, but that is not what I heard. What I heard was "this is my house it's now time for you to leave," and what do you know…. that couple ended up renting that house. So let's jump in and see how can we begin to listen with our hearts more and with our ears less, and how can we start to hear the difference between intent and content. To listen with your heart, first off you have to have an open heart and you also have to understand that the heart is not loud. The heart has very subtle energy with a very subtle voice, just like the voice of your intuition. When you listen with your heart and tune into the heart's energy it releases the tension in your body and it begins to relax you. Once this happens imagine a golden staircase or a golden elevator running from your brain down to your heart. Now imagine yourself entering the golden elevator or going on the staircase entering the golden light and that you're traveling down to your heart. For me personally when I started doing this, it felt like I was dropping down into my heart. This made me feel as if I was on a roller coaster, like when you go up the hill and then you come down. That's how it felt to me, your experience may be different and that is ok because it's your experience. Once you are able to drop into your heart space, this is when you need to be practicing listening with you heart. You can practice by yourself but preferably you can do it with a partner. The partner does not even have to know what you are doing. If you are doing this by yourself however, something that you can do is to go out in public and just listen to what people are saying around you. You should also try to see the intent verses the content in your own voice. Most of us throughout our lives have lied to ourselves. We have said that we are fine or we are okay but in actuality were not so.

You can begin to practice listening with your heart by listening to yourself and seeing what you are really saying to yourself. Now if you'd like to work with a partner all you have to do is ask someone something and listen with your heart, listen to the content not the intent. Don't worry about the question that you are asking, just listen to the voice after you have already asked the question this will be your heart answering. The other thing about this tool is that it may not be words it may just be a feeling and that is perfectly fine. You may be a clairsentient which means you clearly feel with your whole body. As you continue to use this tool your heart will become stronger and stronger and you will become more in tune with your intuitive voice. However just hearing the intent behind someone's voice or behind someone's words is not the full scope of this tool. This tool will help you to tune into yourself, to your heart, which will then help to attune you to your intuition.

This is how I want the universe to treat me!

For some of you as you awaken to your intuition, to your psychic ability, you will start to notice different people, places, and situations falling away because as you awaken to your intuition, things that no longer serve you fade away. Now I have heard of people doing spontaneous awakenings, where their whole entire life falls apart and they lose everything and that's how they awaken to intuition. By no means is that what needs to happen to you to awaken to your intuition. It didn't happen like that for me, mine was completely natural and I am so grateful for that. Yours can be natural to; you don't have to have your life fall apart to awaken to what is already inside of you. Some people have agreed to this type of awakening previously with the soul contract they make before this life begins. They say that is what they need to awaken their intuition. But you are always more than welcome to change that contract. I told the universe a very long time ago that I wanted it to treat me gently and gingerly; I didn't want the universe to come at me so hard to where I had to lose everything just to awaken. I didn't think that was fair nor was it something that I wanted at all so that's why I told the universe "universe please treat me gently and gingerly please give me signs throughout my whole journey and please help me to connect with my guides angels and higher self easily." The funny thing is that's exactly what the universe has done for me. You can also tell the universe how you want to be treated, and how you would like to receive your messages. I have asked the universe for gentle messages and to keep giving them to me until I get the message and until I understand, but never to be harsh about it. I have asked for the universe to just give me gentle reminders, and it has done just that. It's a form of intention and it's a form of affirmation. You are intending that the universe is going to treat you in a certain way and you are making a request. We are trust fund babies of the universe. The universe/God/source will give us whatever we want regardless if it is good for us or bad for us. There are things we want and then spirit says yes and then provides the circumstances to get what we wanted, so if you asked the universe to hit you over the head with a 2 x 4 for your messages, well then guess what, you are going to get hit over the head with a 2 x 4 and that is how you will experience your messages. But you are able to change that and that is the whole point of intention. I had my friend Debbie call me today and she asked me if I remember that old crockpot commercial that said "set it and forget it" I told her no, but she said that we can do that with our intentions .you can set your intention and then you forget it. Set it then forget it and that's basically what you're doing with this tool on how you want the universe to treat you, just say universe I would like you to treat me in this way and then you forget about it and you move on. Then you will see how the universe supports you.

CHAPTER 6

Affirmations and intentions the secret power of your subconscious mind.

Affirmations and intentions are one of the most common spiritual tools you have and it is also one of the hardest to master. You may be asking yourself, why is it so hard to master affirmations and intentions? It's because of the society that we live in. It makes affirmations and intentions so difficult because all too often we have a lot of negative self-talk, which means we talk about ourselves in an extremely negative way. Let's take for example that you messed up on something maybe a project and you say to yourself, "I'm so stupid" and let's face it, we've all said that at one time or another, or we may say I'm so fat or the one that I find most popular is I'm poor; I have no money. These things that you say whether you are serious or just kidding make a difference in your life. It truly does make a difference to your subconscious mind. Your subconscious mind is that part of you that takes those constant affirmations and turns them into beliefs. Once they turn into beliefs, it becomes very hard to change them. Because your subconscious mind has made this a belief, you now think and believe that you are so fat, so stupid, poor, worthless and the list goes on and on it's because of that negative self-talk. Your subconscious mind is like a child, it's always listening and absorbing information. If you constantly say the same thing over and over again, you will begin to believe the things you say about yourself. This is why I believe the ancient people said that words have power because in actuality they do. With affirmations you want to make sure you are affirming what you want and not what you do not want. For example you may say to yourself as you look at your mound of bills, "I'm so poor I don't have enough money to pay for this." It's because of that belief that you have set into yourself, by saying that you do not have enough, that you will never have enough. Then your mind, the creator of your reality, then makes it so you do not have enough, because this is what it now believes and then you never have enough because that is what you have affirmed. That is what you have repeated to yourself so that is what your subconscious mind now believes. Since it is a belief, the universe/God, who always gives you what you want and believe, presents you with the reality you have created; the reality of being poor and unable to pay your bills. So if you want to change that reality, you need to start making affirmations that are going to help you. A great way to start affirmations is of course to state what you want and in a positive way, like you already have it. For example, all my financial and monetary needs are always met. That way you are affirming what you want and that you already have it. another great way to get yourself out of an old belief system when feel stressed anxious or overwhelmed, stop yourself and say "that's not me anymore! I am grateful that I have all the money I need to pay all my bills, buy groceries and I have _____ amount of money left over. I am willing to be surprised at how the universe brings that to me." What you are doing with this affirmation is you are changing your belief about money, once you change your belief and that changes your mind, once you change your mind, you change your reality and you then begin to experience what it is that you truly want in life. Now this by no means is an overnight process. I had to say that affirmation for 30 days and even after that, because I still would have bouts of anxiety about money. Now I know this may seem overwhelming, because it seems as if you have to watch everything you say or think and you do, but you don't have to worry because it's not as hard as it seems. It's merely a matter of paying attention to your thoughts and let's say that you do have a slip where you do say I'm so stupid etc., a great way to clear that out is to simply say, "cancel, clear, delete" and then replace it with "I am the smartest person I know." Affirmations as well as intentions work at a subconscious level so it is also good to have visuals such as a vision board. This way your subconscious mind, which does act on visual stimuli, can see it as well. What I believe the most important part about affirmations is the fact that you have to believe in the affirmation that you are saying. If you don't believe it, then it doesn't matter how many times you say it, how many different ways you put it, you still will not get your desired result from the affirmation that you are saying, because you do not believe it. Since you do not believe it, your subconscious mind doesn't either, that's the trick with affirmations as well as intentions. You have to believe in them, you have to believe that what you are saying is possible. Without the belief then as I said, it doesn't matter if you say the affirmations for one day, 30 days, or even 100 days, you will not see your desired result. So how do you solve the problem of believing in your affirmations and intentions? What I suggest is that you start small with something you know you can change. So let's say that you drink a lot of caffeinated drinks and you would like to stop that, so go ahead and come up with an affirmation for cutting caffeine out of your diet. You know it's believable and you know you can do it. It's just a matter of doing it and don't set yourself up for failure by saying an affirmation that you do not believe in, or setting an intention you don't believe will come into manifestation. Just start small and then you can get bigger and bigger with your affirmations and intentions. I do recommend saying affirmations for 30 days at minimum. What that does, is it puts it into your mind and makes it a habit by you saying it, because it does take about 21 days to start a habit. Another great practice for affirmations and intentions is to make short little ones that you can repeat throughout the day. You can say them in the morning, the afternoon, at night and throughout the day. You could just start off saying one affirmation. Let's say that you have very low self-esteem, now what you can begin to say is, "I speak my truth boldly and bravely" very simple, sweet and to the point, then you can start to add in more affirmations from there. How do you know when you no longer need to say an affirmation? The best way you can tell that you no longer need to say an affirmation is because you are doing what you have already affirmed and it becomes natural for you to do it. You don't have to say the affirmation and you are just able to do it. So let us use again the example of money, you come across a bill and it is for far more than you had budgeted for. Instead of stressing out, you just breathe and have a knowing that it is going to be taken care of. Now if you still feel the need to say the affirmation, because the anxiety is building up and you at the first glance were absolutely fine go ahead and say the affirmation again. Now let's move on to intentions. Affirmations and intentions both work with the subconscious mind, however affirmations is saying the same thing over and over again until it sinks into the subconscious mind. While an intention on the other hand is something that you desire or want in the physical world, so you set the intention for now. What does intention really mean? a thing intended; an aim or plan according to Webster's dictionary. So how do you set intentions? While there are many different ways in which you can set intentions, one of my favorite ways is to write them down. All you need is a piece of paper, a pen, pencil, or any kind of writing utensil and then what you do is write down what it is that you want. For example I intend to get that promotion at work; you are setting your aim, your goal, to get the promotion at work. You are telling the universe that is something that you want. What's hard about intentions is letting them go. You can set them all day long, I intend this, I intend that, but the real hard part of intentions is letting them go. That's how they come into manifestation. That is how they come into physical form. Now you can use the intention and then use an affirmation to assist you, but once again it's really about letting the intention go and giving it to the universe. So what I suggest doing one of two things after you've written down your intention, get a glass bowl or glass cup or anything that is a fireproof and then on the new moon, which is all about sowing the seeds of things that you want, you go outside and you burn that piece of paper. In that ritual act, you are releasing those intentions, those desires, out to the universe so that you can let it go. another great way that you can let go of your intentions is to rip up the piece of paper and just throw it away and then just let it go. Don't think about it at all, just let the universe work out how it is going to happen. That is the other hard part of setting intentions, because our minds always come up with ways that we could do something or have something. But the universe always has a better way for us to obtain what we want. So set the intention and then let it go and don't think about it. A great way to do this is by listening to classical music, no vocals, just the instruments that way your mind is focused on the instrumental on the sound and vibration that each instrument makes. It allows you to slip in the sound, to an altered state of consciousness almost like a meditation but not that deep. Now I do encourage you to come up with your own affirmations but if you need help here are 30 affirmations that I have written down to help you get started.

1. I am loved.
2. I am secure.
3. I can do all things through the power of my subconscious
4. I am intuitive.
5. Higher self, I am your faithful servant and I am open to your way.
6. My spirit guides me effortlessly through life.
7. I graciously accept good in my life
8. I release all fears to receiving love.
9. God loves me.
10. I deserve love and assistance.
11. The universe is a source of wealth and it pours upon me.
12. I trust my intuition
13. I listen to my spirit for guidance and assistance.
14. I live from my spirit always.
15. I am open to guidance from my angels and guides.
16. I am a co-creator with the universe and I take full responsibility for all of my creation.

17. I believe in myself and my abilities.

18. I choose happiness, success, and wealth in my life.

19. I am strong.

20. I am healthy and fit.

21. I reach and maintain my ideal goal weight.

22. I am in charge of how I feel and today I choose happiness.

23. I trust the universe to bring the right people and circumstances into my life at the right time.

24. I accept myself.

25. I am grateful.

26. I love and approve of myself

27. I feel the love of those who are not physically around me.

28. I take pleasure in my own solitude.

29. Money comes to me easily and effortlessly.

30. Wealth constantly flows into my life.

CHAPTER 7

Meditation is not a scary word

The M word is a word a lot of people fear. When I say meditation, what was the first thing that comes to your mind? Is it a person with her legs crossed surrounded by candles chanting or do you see someone sitting under a tree that does not seem to be disturbed by anything, including the bugs buzzing around them? Both of those are forms of meditation, but there are many different kinds of meditation. In my personal opinion I believe that there is an infinite number of ways to meditate because there are an infinite number of people in the world. But before we jump into meditation let me give you a little information about it. First Webster's dictionary describes meditation as the act or instance of planning or thinking quietly. What I would like you to do right now is think about if you have ever tried to plan something out in your head, well then guess what, that was a form of meditation. Have you ever tried to plan something while out walking? That is also a form of meditation. What about when you are so entranced in an activity maybe dancing, exercising or singing that you've just stopped thinking altogether yes, you guessed it, that's another form of meditation. Science has proven that meditation is great for you physically as well as mentally Harvard did a study and it showed that people that meditate, at least people that meditate once a day, are actually growing back gray matter in the brain. Meditation can also speed up your brain's processing potential. Meditation on a regular basis can loosen up or lessen our feelings of anxiety, because of the neural pathways linking our Me Center to our fear decreases. Basically the anxiety becomes regulated and it is easy for new neural pathways to form. Another interesting fact is that meditation can reduce the risk of heart disease. In a study done in 2012, 201 people with coronary heart disease were given a choice to either take a health class promoting improved diet or take a transcendental meditation class over the course of the research. Over five years of this research and they discovered that those who chose the option to the transcendental meditation class had a 48% reduction in their overall risk: so as you can see meditation has a lot of physical benefits.

So you may be asking yourself how do I meditate and what's the best way to meditate? Well the only way to find out the best meditation style for you is to try out different ones. Now I don't mean to try one for just a day; I don't even mean for a week. I would like for you to do, is to try different forms of meditation and try them for two weeks at a time. The first week is going to get you used to meditating in a particular style, while the second week you'll be getting the hang of it and be able to see if it's really working for you. I will tell you that my favorite way to meditate is to go on a nature walks. I am very blessed to live in a neighborhood that actually has a park in the very center of it and it has a beautiful wooded area where I am able to go and walk. What I do is I simply set the intention for something that I need clarity on. Let's say that I need to make a job decision so I set the intention to gain clarity on that specific area in my life, then I take a deep breath and I begin to walk. Thoughts of my intention may still pop up in my mind and I continue to walk until I stop thinking or until the only thing that I hear or that I am aware of is either my feet walking or my breath going in and out. If I am still becoming distracted, I just focus on the beautiful nature all around me and as I do that, my subconscious mind takes over and allows my guides or angels to help me come up with a solution. Sometimes I don't even set an intention. I just go and walk that is what I like to call a "no mind" meditation. This meditation is great to do if you have had a stressful day at work, home, or you just have a lot to think about. This meditation can be done on a walk or while listening to music. All you have to do is focus on your breathing. I like to imagine all the breath entering my heart so that way I can get out of my head and I give my brain a break. This meditation I find is also good for connecting with your guides and angels, because it gets your ego out of the way of your conscious mind, your rational mind.

Another meditation you can do is of course a guided meditation and there are hundreds of thousands of them on YouTube and the Internet. I even have some on my YouTube channel; (Ronald Schaefer). The guided meditations that I have on my channel are ones to meet your guides and also a new moon meditation along with several others. Why is meditation so important? Meditation is very important because it allows you to get out of your head and it allows you to tap into your subconscious mind as well as your heart. It starts to help you balance between the hemispheres of your brain and also creates balance between your head and your heart. Meditation also allows you to connect with the more subtle energies of your guides and angels as well as your own intuitive voice and your higher self. For me I like to meditate once a day for an hour. For most people just starting to meditate I recommend just trying it for five minutes once a day. I have some strategies for you to start meditating, some of these tips are my own and some I have learned over the years from others spiritual teachers. The first tip I think is one of the most important and it is to have no expectation of how long your meditation will be, also not to have an expectation of the experience that you will have. No one is going to have the same experience we all have different experiences, because we all have different perceptions and views. If you set an expectation up and you do not get what you expected, then you may not want to meditate anymore because you didn't get your desired result. So know that your first time meditating you may not get to see or hear your guides, and or you may not get to see your angels. You may experience nothing at all and that is absolutely fine. You just need to honor that and know that it's okay.

The next thing I want to point out is exactly what I pointed out in the first part of this chapter, that there are so many different ways to meditate, so if one way does not work for you then it's totally fine. You may even start to fuse some different ways together if you think that that will help you. Another great tip that I learned is trying to come up with a time that you know you're going to be able to sit down and meditate. Try to make it the same time every day this way your body and mind get used to the routine of meditating at a certain time, so that all your biological processes begin to slow down and your mind begins to calm as you get closer to the time of your meditation. You also want to make sure that you have a quiet space to meditate just for you, even if that place is in the car. I know for me personally when I was trying to find a time to meditate it was difficult because we were in the car an awful lot driving back and forth to work, picking people up from work because we only had one car. So I couldn't really find a place to meditate except in the car. When I would get in the car there would be music playing the majority of the time so I would lower it a little bit and I would then begin my meditation. it would just be for a quick five minutes and that was okay because at least I was able to meditate for that five minutes. Sometimes I would even wait until everyone got out of the car and then I would meditate for 5 to 10 minutes that always seem to work a lot better. A great way to meditate in your car is to simply put your palms facing up on your knees, make sure your back is straight and as you breathe in say to yourself "I am" then as you breathe out say, "calm." So again on the inhale you say, "I am" and on the exhale you say, "Calm." Continue this pattern for 5 to 10 minutes.

Meditation after you get used to it, will become your golden time. It will become the time that you look forward to and it will be refreshing. If however you are like my friend Kim and your mind likes to wander regardless of what you seem to do there are other tips and tools. Like when it continues to wander as you are sitting down trying to quiet your mind, even after saying I am calm and you still have funny pictures, words, or you start to think about what you have to do during the rest of the day. One great tool that I found helpful with this is to imagine a bulldozer pushing the thoughts and pictures in your mind away before you start meditating. Another tool for when I just can't seem to stop the fonts is to imagine a force field or a wall that stopped those thoughts I have even imagined bubbles going around my thoughts and having them flow out of my head. One of the most important things to remember about meditating and psychic energy is that it can't be confined to just one way, so experiment with it. The different ways that I have listed are just scratching the surface of meditation. There are so many different kinds so just go out and try some to find your way of meditating.

So we have found that meditation has a lot of physical benefits to it, meditation is not complicated and it is not hard. What makes it hard, are our brains due to the society that we live in, because we are constantly on the go. We have lifestyles that demand our constant attention. We have phones, laptops, and tablets dinging and screaming for us to look at them. You really just have to make the time to sit and be quiet. The Dalai Lama even says that the greatest meditation sometimes is sleep, so as we have said before you can set the intention to work through a certain situation through your sleep that is yet another form of meditation. The last thing that I want to express in this chapter about meditation is that you have to respect yourself, if you can only do five minutes then that's okay you can only do five minutes. Don't worry you will build up to longer periods of time; it's just a matter of practice. Don't try to make yourself meditate longer then you're able to either, because believe you me it doesn't work. I've tried and all that seems to happen is thoughts start coming into your mind and you can't stop them because your mind is ready to go. Once you come out of the meditation, it's very hard to get yourself back in it. So just respect yourself and be patient with yourself, know that you will get it and know that it's okay. I'm sending you all my love.

CHAPTER 8

Validate your Own Parking

This may seem like a funny title in a book about awakening your intuition. What does validating your own parking have anything to do with intuition; surprisingly it has a lot to do with it. Let me explain, you may have had to have your parking validated before. But what is that validation for? Well to say yes, you can park there that you have permission to do so. In this chapter we are going to be talking about validating your own psychic abilities not your vehicle. Yes as a sensitive, psychic, or intuitive however you wish to refer to yourself as, you have to validate your ability and you cannot depend on others to do that for you. If you do wait for others to validate your abilities, then you will begin to spiral down. Believe me I spiraled very far down, because I doubted myself in the beginning of my psychic journey. I'd given readings to my friends and family and they were dead on and very accurate, so why did I doubt myself? Because I had never actually done it for money and I had never read anyone who was not a friend. I remember my very first reading, I was so nervous to see if I could really pick up on someone else's energy. Like I said I had done it for my friends and family, but weren't they just helping me, being supportive and trying to instill me with self-confidence? All of these thoughts were running through my head. The second thing was I did not want to disappoint my client and I did not want her to waste her $20 because that's all I charged. Lastly I was so nervous I would not be able to connect with her or her guide or angels, that I would be wrong and she would say that

I was a fake or a phony. I was so crazed that day all I can remember is sitting in meditation pleading with the Angels to please help me with this reading to please give me all the right answers to make sure that I gave this client exactly what she needed. I remember as I was driving and still asking my angels and guides to assist me with the reading. This was such a big step for me doing this reading not only for money but also in public and also letting people know online on Facebook that I was a psychic and I was doing readings. I was going to meet the client at the library. We were going to do the reading in one of the rooms the library had provided. Normally these rooms are just a door a table and some chairs well our library went through a renovation and all of the rooms were glass. They still had the tables and chairs but there was no longer any privacy. I got to the library early and got us a room in the back but it really didn't matter because like they said it was all glass so everyone could see exactly what we were doing. So as I was sitting in the room asking for guidance and protection scared to my very core, while needless to say when my phone buzzed with a message from my client telling me that she was here I jumped about 5 feet into the air. I ran quickly out to the lobby and brought her back to the room with me and I gave her a brief synopsis on what the reading was going to entail and then I started. The reading went great and I told her everything I had seen including what was on the cards and when I asked if it was right, I got an immediate yes after each one. She had said that she was amazed especially for my first reading and that she thought that I had been doing it for years. She gave me the money and thanked me. I also was surprised at myself that I was able to give her a message from her grandmother right before we left, but I didn't get a chance to ask if the information was correct. So all night long I thought about it and it kept swirling in my head was that message right? Did I tell her good information? Was it really her grandmother that came through? All night it was driving me crazy I kept asking myself the same questions. The next morning I had a text message from her and it confirmed that the message from her grandmother was absolutely right. she apologized for not telling me right then and there, she was just so shocked from the message that she forgot to tell me. I told her it was not a problem and appreciated her feedback. Now by no means am I telling you not to ask for validation during your reading, because you do need them to make sure that you are connecting with the person's energy. But what I am saying is that you cannot obsess about being right. I remember my spiritual mentor Sonja, she had a client come to her and all Sonja could see was broken glass the girl and her friend at Sonja's table were heckling, her telling her that she was a fake and a phony. Well it just so happens that her grandfather who had died owned a glass factory and that's what the broken glass was in reference to. What I am saying is you cannot obsess about being right. If you obsess about being right, then that's when you begin to spiral downwards and that's when you have to start validating yourself. If you don't validate yourself, then you're never going to be able to move forward, you're going to constantly second-guess yourself and your intuition. Which then will not be good for your clients, because you'll never really know if you're giving them accurate information? You'll never trust what's coming through and that is the very basis of psychic abilities as well as intuition. You have to trust the messages you receive. My friend Marianne, an amazing Akashic reader like myself, once had to tell a client pudding pie. She didn't know what it meant. She just knew she had to say it and when she did it was perfect confirmation to a client of hers that it was in fact her grandmother coming through. After that first reading I went on to do even more readings and I still was asking constantly for validation. One day a friend of mine contacted me and said she would like for me to read a friend of hers, actually two friends. I said fine and I went over to the friend's house. The two ladies I was going to read for were extremely sweet and nice. They offered me water and snacks. After explaining what the reading would entail what she may feel or what may happen, I began the reading and I started to do the cards as I did and flip them over. I was waiting for the validation the "oh my gosh, how did you know that," or "yes, that's so right." But nothing not even a smile or smirk. I asked does that make sense and I would only get a head nod or a yeah, not at all what I was used to. So I went deeper into spirit trying to get more info so I could get the validation and reaction I so desperately wanted, but I never got it. She paid me and said thank you and I went home worried the whole time. What did she think, was it good or not, then self-doubt started and then I even felt bad she paid me. I felt bad for taking the money from her. I was going crazy. I was about to text her and ask what she thought of the reading, and just as I picked up my phone a text came through. It was her telling me how great the reading was and how she was going to recommend me to all of her friends. I was so grateful that came through, but then I started to wonder why was I so obsessed with being right. Why was it so important for me to get validation, why did I need it from her? Then I realized it was my ego that needed it, that craved it. After that I decided I was going to validate myself. But how can I do that without asking if the information I was giving was correct? One way I started to do this was by getting a small pocket notebook and when I would get intuitive messages I would write it down and date it. Then when my gut feeling or intuitive vibe came, I was able to pick up on someone's mood and then later they came and confessed how they felt to me. I was validated but I did not seek the validation. The validation came to me. Another way I found to help me gain more self-confidence was to give readings, cold readings. I would just go to one of my coworkers or close friends who I trusted and say I would like to give you a reading. I also did this with my best friends as well which helped me gain more confidence in myself. I also use affirmations to help me gain more confidence. The one I used was "I have a strong intuitive voice. I freely receive guidance and I accept and trust the messages I receive." After a couple of months I felt better. I still was scared but I no longer let the fear control me. I didn't need others to validate my abilities or the information that I gave. I no longer had the overwhelming desire or need to be validated. Now by no means does this mean I have completely conquered it, because I still have my bouts of self-doubt but at least now I know how to control it.

CHAPTER 9

There is No Light without Shadow and No Shadow without Light.

In the previous chapter you read about my struggle with self-confidence. This is a form of what we are going to talk about in this chapter, which is shadow work. What is shadow work? It is in a sense what we do not like about ourselves, for me my shadow work was working on my self-confidence but also it was about abandonment of family and friends. Shadow work came up for me in 2013 during Mercury Retrograde (Mercury retrograde is when the planet Mercury appears to be rotating backwards.) During Mercury retrograde depending on your astrological chart you may experience a lack of communication, confusion, and or malfunctioning of electronics. Electronics not work properly is just the beginning of things that may happen during a Mercury retrograde.

What happened to me was I was working in my classroom on our professional development day. On professional development days we are given the opportunity to be inside our classrooms and clean as well as come up with new curriculum. This was a very different professional development day, because usually we go to a larger center but we were able to work in our own rooms at our own centers. This year on our professional development day it was all about cleaning. I was working in the classroom with two wonderful ladies, at this point I will just call them Kim, who I shared all my psychic/intuitive information with & NJ who I did not because of her religious beliefs and she had asked me not to share them with her. I went in and we were cleaning NJ's favorite thing to do. Kim had come in and told me about a rough emotional weekend she had. She also told me that as she was driving in Noblesville, which is where I live, the song Happy came on and that she looked up and said "thanks Ron!" as if I had turned the song on for her. She knew that that was my favorite song and we talked about what had happened over the weekend. Then when NJ interrupted it started to feed the fire of Kim's bad mood. while I was on the other side of the room cleaning I started to pick up on the negative vibes and me being the person that I am went over and tried to change it all over to a more positive note. It was working but once again NJ came over and started to bring Kim down yet again. I remembered what my spiritual role model Sonja had said that if people are being negative, the best thing that you can do is to use your left and right foot and just walk away so that is exactly what I did. I walked to the other side of the room and I started to clean again. However it didn't really seem to matter, I could hear what they were talking about and I was still listening to them. I tried to tune them out, but our radio had broken so there was no music in our room so I could just hear them talking about how terrible their lives were and it was actually bringing me down. Now I had started to think negatively. I started to think about how I was not invited to a staff party because it was only for women. I am the only male working there and I started to think about how that wasn't fair. The day started to become more and more negative and I felt myself move out of my spirit and move into my ego. I once again tried to go over and tried to dissolve the negative energy, but at this point there was no use because now I was in that negative energy with them. We were all becoming more and more negative. The space began to get darker and darker and it even seemed that the sun was getting darker because of the bad mood we were all emitting. NJ then told me as I was trying to bring their moods up, that I was not helping, that I did not understand girls feelings, and that I didn't understand feelings at all. Well this was the wrong thing to say to an empathic spiritual intuitive who feels things very deeply and not to mention to say it during Mercury retrograde. Needless to say I took this wrong and it hit a cord in me, a very deep cord. How dare she say that I didn't feel and how dare she think that she understands things more than me! I was moving into my ego and fast. I basically just ended the conversation by walking away. I started cleaning, trying to just get out of my own mind but NJ was not done. She continued to passive aggressively attack me from across the room. She kept asking me, "Did I make you mad? Did I make you mad? Did I make you mad?" finally I blew up and said, "yes you did make me mad and I don't appreciate what you said. I am a human being and I have feelings too. I understand feelings probably more than you do." She then tried to soften it up with; "you don't understand *girl's* feelings, that's all I was trying to say." It didn't matter because I was emanating anger and I blocked out anything that she was saying. So what I did was I walked away pretended to go get more chemicals for cleaning but in reality I'd walked over to a coworker in another room who I've known for five years. I asked her if I could have a hug really quick and she told me sure. As her arms embraced me I laid my head on her shoulder, and I began to burst into tears. She asked me what was wrong and I told her that Kim and NJ were just being so negative and I was so sad that I was not invited to her party. I didn't understand why I couldn't come and I didn't understand why Kim was siding with NJ. I just didn't understand and I just cried for a good five minutes uncontrollably until I got my wits about me. Then I took a deep breath I told my friend I was so sorry for doing that. She said that it was fine and that's what friends are for; we're here to support and help each other that are what friends do. I shook my head and she told me in the nicest way "Honey you stay with me, don't go back to those bitches, they do nothing but pull you down." She then told me "they are not worth your time anyway." I agreed so I stayed in the room with my coworker who I've known for five years and I helped her clean. I was very quiet as I was internalizing all of my emotions at that time, still trying to understand and comprehend how someone could be so mean. Then it was time for lunch. We all met in the prekindergarten room Kim and NJ were sitting together and still in their negative moods. I wanted nothing to do with them. I actually went to go eat in a whole other room by myself so I would not have to look at them. The day passed and I left completely drained emotionally.

The next day I had decided that I was going to be extremely passive aggressive towards Kim. I did things that I know that she does not like such as bossing her around, telling her what to do, and telling her what time we were going to do it at. She hated all of those things but she was doing the same thing to me. she was being extremely passive aggressive in the way that she would answer me in a very short and sarcastic tone. All through that day however I felt my intuitive voice telling me that something was all wrong. it wasn't until the other teacher who was with us had talked about a shooting that happened when Kim then revealed to us that one of her friends she knew in high school had actually died in that. I told her I was sorry for her loss and I gave her a hug. She said it was okay that she hadn't seen this friend over five years. I finally broke down and told her that I was mad at her. I didn't know why I was mad at her and as I talked about it, I found no reason to be mad at her. She told me the exact same thing that she was mad at me and didn't know why either. We were both just angry. We laughed about it, gave each other hugs, and said we were sorry for being assholes to each other and being passive aggressive.

NJ came in about two hours after Kim and I had made up but as soon as I saw NJ, I immediately became angry again. I couldn't understand why and then all of a sudden it hit me. It was because NJ was the antagonist. NJ was taking my friend away from me. She tried to give me a hug and tell me she was sorry and I accepted it but not fully. I just couldn't so I had to find out why was I still so angry. I went into meditation and I got very quiet and I asked why I am still angry at NJ. All of a sudden a vision of me as a child came up with my siblings telling me that I wouldn't have any friends. Then another vision of me sitting alone at a lunch table and even more visions of me being isolated and alone not having any friends. My siblings told me all the time at that very young age that I didn't have any friends and that I never would. That became a belief and so when I finally made real friends I was holding onto them for dear life. NJ became a threat to me losing a friend that I was very close to. That's why I was so upset with her. That's why I couldn't forgive her because she was the living embodiment of what I feared the most. She was going to take away something precious to me, something I had worked so hard to get, a real friend.

This took months of digging really deep and forgiving a lot of different people until I was finally able to forgive NJ. but I needed to keep searching what part of me, what part of my life made me feel like I did not matter and that people around me were not my friends. This process took several months however after I had dealt with it, I was able to not only to move forward but also to learn and grow as a person. This is just one part of shadow work, which is to forgive the people involved but also to forgive yourself. I have found this affirmation very helpful I forgive _____ I release him/her mentally and spiritually. I completely forgive everything connected to this matter in question. I am free; you or she is free and it is a marvelous feeling, today is my day of general amnesty.

Another affirmation that I have used is I release anybody and everyone who has ever hurt me and I wish for each and every one of them health, happiness, peace and all the blessings of life. I do this freely, and joyfully. How will you know what your shadow work is? How will you be able to know when you have entered into shadow work? Well one way to find out what your shadow work is by getting a deck of Oracle cards. In your deck what I would like for you to do is find the card that you like the most; the card that when it comes out in a reading you get excited. Now look for the card that is your least favorite the one when it comes up you groan or you don't want to see. After you do that, look at both your favorite card and look at all the different shades colors look at what you like about the card, then look at the second card and do the exact same thing. Determine what you don't like about that card and what turns you off about that card. The first card is where you want to head in life the second card is your shadow work. This is what you fear or you need to work on. After you find out what your shadow work is there are tons of ways in which you can deal with your personal shadow work. One way is through meditation and getting very quiet and asking yourself where you were hurt where did this come from. Another great one is to write down the word shadow work and then all the different things attributed with what you don't like about yourself. I actually watched a video on YouTube that helped me it was by a lady named Teal Scott. However no one can tell you what is the best way for you to do your shadow work, because it's your personal journey into changing the things you don't like about yourself. Shadow work can seem very scary and a daunting task. On some levels it is, however once you come out of it, you are stronger, wiser and have a better understanding of yourself. As I said in the chapter title you have to accept the darkness with the light for if you deny that part of you, you can never really be a whole person and cannot move beyond your current place or situation. That part of you will persist. So my dear love, it is time for you to delve into the shadows and come out an even brighter light. I'm sending you all my love.

Section1
Angles and Guides

In the first part of the chapter we discussed a lot of inner work, and here in section one we are going to be discussing the entities and tools that you can use in the physical world. The first thing I want to say is that none of these beings will do the work for you. They will point things out for you and they will guide you, but they will not do it for you, which is why they are called guides. In saying that, I would like to explain my view on these beings. First yes, they are in a sense outside of you, because they are in other dimensions and other frequencies, but at the same time they are a part of you. In my view, angels and guides are different multidimensional beings or aspects of you, and as you grow and evolve so do they. That is why you have so many guides that come in and out of your life. Now you do have four guides that stay with you your whole life. These guides are your core, and they work with you the most and will gain the greatest evolution as you continue to evolve in your own consciousness. The same rings true of angels. You have guardian angels and most people have two. There is your introverted angel, who strokes her aura, and makes you feel calm or love. Then you have your extroverted Angel. This is the one who gives you messages and guides you and protects you in the physical now. There are many different guides and angels, whom we will talk about throughout this chapter and throughout the book. Guides and angels are your invisible support team. They give you guidance and support in the nonphysical, in the way of signs and symbols. They will also let you know when there is a better way to go or do something. I once again want to reiterate before we go more in depth that spirit guides, angels, ascended masters will never tell you what to do. They will never tell you anything negative; such as you are stupid, I hate you, how dumb can you be, you should go hurt that person or you should hurt yourself. Those are not things that your loving guides, angels, or ascended Masters would ever tell you. If you ever do get an entity like this, please immediately disconnect yourself from it and ask Archangel Michael to cut that cord so it can no longer return. Then ask Archangel Zadileil and ascended master Saint Germaine to use the Violet flame and clear you as well.

CHAPTER 10

It's time to choose a card

Next we are going to be discussing entities and tools that you can use in the physical world and the first I would like to introduce you to the wonderful world of Tarot and Oracle cards. Tarot is a word that has turned a lot of people off because it has had negative connotations to it, but there is nothing to be afraid of. What you have seen on TV like an old gypsy woman telling a young man he is going to die that night and then that night the man gets into a terrible car accident and dies is not realistic and not the real use of cards. The cards are tools that can help you to gain a better understanding through spirit. It's actually called divination and has been a common practice around the world for many centuries. It is only now been given a bad name by TV personalities and or TV shows.

Let's dive into the cards for a moment. The names and scenes on the cards are archetypes just displaying different parts of life and different kinds of people that you may come into contact with in your life. Let's take for example the Queen of pentacles which is a woman of work capable and practical. That's what the card means in the traditional sense. Let us also take the most common misunderstood card of them all in the whole deck, at least in my opinion, the death card. When that comes up in a reading people instantly react with a sense of horror. They always ask, "Am I going to die?" and my answer is always the same. No, the death card is not telling you that you are going to die, the death card mostly is foretelling of transformation; a letting go of things. Yes in essence it is a death, but not a physical death. It's more like something old is leaving your life, so something new can come in. I also tell them that the death card has to be in a very specific spread and in a very specific position for it to mean a physical death. I tell people that I do not do those kinds of readings.

The tarot is a very old form of divination which means the practice of seeking knowledge of the future by supernatural means. Tarot has been around for thousands of years and there are many different decks for you to work with out there. The oldest deck and most notable is the Rider Waite Deck which is what you may find in your local New Age store. Now since tarot has been around for thousands of years, there is a lot of negative press. There are those that think it is taboo or seen as devil worship. Let me assure you this is simply not true. If you are using them to do readings for example to see if your friends finances are going to work out, or if you should take a job opportunity, there is nothing to worry about. There's no fire, brimstone or devils that you're summoning you're simply tapping into the universal field and being given an answer through the archetype of the cards. I want to assure you there's nothing to worry about if you go with the Tarot deck.

Now that we have a little background information on the deck I would like to tell you about my very first deck I worked with and personally the Tarot cards were not for me. Why was the Tarot not for me? The very simple answer to that is that the tarot gives you information like it is. There are no gentle energies. Let me put it in another way, it's like you have a very loud and blunt friend who just tells it like it is. There's no softening the blow or giving you advice on how to fix it. It's more like here is the information and that's it. I will say it was very accurate and is a great way to work on your shadow work, but as I have said it was not for me. However through working with the deck I learned great spreads: such as the cross of truth, the life spread and the traditional Celtic cross. I also learned which court cards represent which zodiac signs. Lastly a great thing that I learned was a way to determine if something was a definite yes or no, so it did teach me a lot. It also showed me that I needed something softer, something that would help me get past the shadows. This led me to Oracle cards for unlike the traditional tarot deck, they range from extremely gentle to not so gentle, but never at the level of the tarot. Oracle cards to me are if I may give another example, like your grandma giving you advice by restating the problem you have and then giving you advice on that problem and or how to fix it for yourself.

Just like the tarot you have different ways you can lay out the cards known as spread, which represent past, present, and future or a Celtic cross like in the tarot. However the great thing about Oracle cards is that you have a little more freedom to come up with your own spread, which you can also do in the tarot but as I said Oracle cards do not have that restrictive dogma as the tarot does. Just like the tarot the Oracle cards are just archetypes of the energies that you are working with. It's another theme represented through pictures. Oracle cards I feel you get more out of the cards because as I have already stated there is no dogma like in the tarot, you have more freedom to look at the different signs and symbolism of the card. My favorite example of this is Doreen virtues Ascended Master Cards. These cards are just pictures of the ascended Masters, however if you look close, she has put some surprises in there. For example the pan card, I have never noticed the flowers or the girl dancing in the background and it was not until I put it on my altar that I noticed those things.

So what I would like to do is to look at your cards to see what little details you find, remember it is on the card for a reason. With each deck I get, I take it home and as soon as I take it out of the box I hit the front of the cards then the back of the cards and I shake the deck with my dominant hand. Why I do this is because I am getting anyone else's energy that has come in contact with those cards off, so the cards are only picking up on my energy. I also would recommend smudging or saging your cards (Sage is a herb that is naturally grown. it is said to have the metaphysical properties of a cleansing or clearing negative energy from people objects or environments.) You can also use salt. Salt is a natural neutralizer of energy both positive and negative. Something else I like to do is to put my cards in direct sunlight and I set the intention that the sun is going to clean and clear them and also entwine them with universal truth and knowledge. What I like to do after that is I shake them once more, then I put the deck in my dominant hand and I take my non-dominant hand and bring it to my heart chakra in the middle of my chest. I then gently bless the cards with a sweeping motion saying love three times over the left side, then the right side, then the top, then the bottom, then the back and then I repeat this with the words of wisdom, truth, compassion, and light and whatever else I would like to entwine into the cards. My very good friend Debbie B. likes to sleep with her cards underneath her pillow. That is something she does to put her energy onto the cards. There are multiple ways for you to put your energy on the cards. The ways that I have told you are just a few suggestions that I have used. You are more than welcome to use your own ways.

Now let's get to the fun part. Take your cards in your non-dominant hand, then with your dominant hand pick up a small section and move it to the front or the back and continue to do this with a faster and faster pace until the cards begin to pop out. Something fun that you can do with each of your decks is to find your signifier card. Now your signifier card is the card that best represents your energy, this is going to be the card that when you pull it is going to represent you. Personally this is one of my favorite things to do with a new deck of cards to see what card best represents my energy. It is very simple all you have to do is get quiet in your mind and hold the cards in your non-dominant hand and simply ask what card best represents my energy at this time? Then you begin to shuffle whatever cards or card that pops out is the card that best represents your energy at this time. I recommend doing readings for yourself first, before moving on to family and friends I say this so that you can start to understand what the cards mean to you. Of course you are more than welcome to use the guidebook, but you may also see things in the cards that may stand out to you that have no definition within the guidebook.

I like to say a prayer before I start any reading which is very short and sweet and to the point, I ask for guidance and protection during this reading and then I state the person's name. Then I begin to shuffle or tune into the energy, if I don't have cards. There is general maintenance for your cards. After I do readings with people I like to cleanse and clear my cards. Once again you can use the Sage, sunlight, moonlight, salt or whatever cleansing method you find works best for you. Maintenance is needed because your cards pick up the energy of the people around you or other people you read for. You want to get a clear reading for each person that you are reading, so that is why when I do my readings if I am doing multiples I always hit the front and back of the cards and then shake them to release that persons energy from the cards. Also it's best to keep your cards in a high-energy area. Mine are not on my altar but they are underneath it in a drawer. If you don't have one, it's not a problem just keep them in a place were not a lot of people are going to go. If you don't have that luxury, then you can do what my friend Debbie does and just place them in your bed that way they are always absorbing your energy.

CHAPTER 11

Angles and Guides True connection.

When first trying to connect with your guides or angels, it can be very frustrating. I know for me it was. I think I tried at least six or seven types of meditation at least 30 different videos to try and get in contact with my own personal guides and angels and there was no communication. After the first month I was beginning to think that I did not have angels or guides, however I had watched so many videos saying that everyone does I was really at a loss. I did not know what to do. I thought well I guess I do not have any or maybe I am just not that gifted, or maybe I'm not reaching out to my guides correctly. Both of these thoughts saddened me and disheartened me. Since I wasn't being able to connect, I went to a psychic and asked if I have guides or angels. This psychic looked at me with a very puzzled look and said "yes, they been talking to you for months." I said well I have not heard them for months. He then gave me a description of them. I was so happy and elated and I was also relieved. He said that they were always around me and always wanting to talk to me every time I asked a question. He gave me the questions that I had asked them and then the answers that they had relayed to him. I had a renewed sense of hope.

I was going to try again and I was going to connect with my guides and angels. So I set out on my quest to connect with my guides and angels. For about two weeks, I did meditation after meditation, psychic development exercise, after psychic development exercise, doing my hardest to connect with my guides but no matter what I was doing I just couldn't do it. I pleaded every day for them to come but no signs or symbols, just nothing. Then one day I was talking on a Google hang out with a psychic group that I am a part of. The topic incidentally was guides and angels. I had gotten a reading a very long time ago from the leader of the group, so I knew she was amazing. Near the end I asked why are my guides not coming through and explained that I had done all the exercises and meditations but still nothing. She told me that basically I was not allowing my guides in. I laughed at her and said what do you mean not allowing them in?? I call on them every day and I ask to work with them every day, but they are the ones who are not coming to me. She smiled very gently at me and said, "Ron you are calling on them, but you are not allowing them to guide you. You are expecting them to come in a certain way and when they don't, you get disappointed. Your guides have been sending you signs for months, and you just haven't been paying attention." I thought about it and I guess that she was right. She said that basically I needed to call them into my auric field and allow them to come in there. Otherwise it was like they were screaming at me from across the football field, hence why couldn't hear them or see their signs. So I started to invite my guides into my auric field. I was sitting in meditation it was a meditation I had done before so I could tell when the meditation was coming to an end. As I got into an extremely quiet place, all of a sudden a man in flowing white robes came up to me. He was about arm's length away. He was a white man in his mid-20s, he had a buzz cut, and the kindest eyes I had ever seen. I could not see his body because of the flowing robes all around him. I asked, "Who are you?" and I heard a gentle whisper say Benjamin. Then all of a sudden a golden bird appeared on his finger and then the bird flew over to me and landed on my finger. I looked back and the man was gone and then I looked at the bird and it was gone, and right before the meditation ended I heard the words golden finch. My very first reaction was OMG what was that? Who was that? What just happened? Right after that my immediate reaction was to go look up the word golden finch and when I did it meant celebration/meeting new people. I thought who did I just meet? A random entity name Benjamin? Then all of a sudden the thought came into my head, guardian angel. I said to myself OMG I just met my guardian angel. But did I really or was it just wishful thinking. I mean it was extremely vivid but had I actually met my personal guardian angel? What I did was I asked for a sign in the physical world to let me know that that interaction I had was real. The next day I went on my walk as I normally do and all of a sudden the bird I had seen in my meditation flew by me not once, but twice. I thought to myself, was that my sign or should I be looking for something else? I didn't know so I asked again for a sign. The next day when I went on my walk two birds that I had seen in my meditation flew by me, now I thought okay that's my sign. Wow I really did meet my guardian angel. Then I guess since I kept on asking for a sign my guardian angel decided to be funny, because angels have a sense of humor. at least in my opinion they do and the next day when I went for my walk, not one or even two finches but five golden finches flew past me. Which in the state of Indiana where I live, they are on the endangered species list so I was doubly amazed that I saw five of them. Altogether I had seen eight of them; I was in shock and awe. So that was my experience with getting in touch with my angels and guides or at least with my guardian angel. My guides were much easier after I got in touch with my guardian angel.

The first guide I came in contact with was my wolf guide and he also came in during meditation. All I saw of him was his darting yellow eyes and it also happened right before the meditation was over. I again wanted to make sure that had actually happened so once again I asked for a sign in the physical world. Two days later I received it by seeing a wolf on TV, a wolf in a magazine then a wolf in a book my sister had brought home. I was seeing wolves everywhere. I understood that this was also one of my guides and after our first interaction I was able to connect with that wolf even more, and as I did my other guides began to come in and I was able to work with them as well. So the gateway for me was my guardian angel. This doesn't mean that your guardian angel will be the gateway for you to meet your other guides and spiritual helpers. You may have very powerful guides that want to speak with you first before your guardian angel, or you may be like me and have a very strong connection to the angelic realm, so it's much easier for you to connect with your guardian angel. Whatever the case may be, know that it is going to take time and to have patience with yourself to connect with your guides.

I would like to give you some tips and tools that you can use to better connect with your guardian angel and guides. The first thing is of course what I have already stated which is asking for a sign in the physical world that your guides or angels are with you. You are more than welcome to give them a time limit. I like to usually set the limit for three days by setting the intention that you will receive a message in the physical world from your guides and angels within the three days. If you cannot get in contact with them through meditation another great way is to ask your angels for an Angel number. What is an Angel number? An Angel number is a set of numerical patterns of repeating digits for example 444 or 363 or 557 all of these are Angel numbers these numbers for me show up on license plate, receipts or totals that I owe on something that I have just purchased. You can ask yourself what does it mean to you and see if you get any response from your guides or angels if not there is a great website that you can go to help you find out what these numbers mean. http://sacredscribesangelnumbers.blogspot.com/p/index-numbers. html This website is absolutely amazing and I am in love with the woman who did it. she did such a wonderful job of transcribing all the different Angel numbers, and not only that she also tells you what each individual number means 1through 10 as well. even though this is a great website remember you cannot rely on others interpretations because their perception and your words are different, so by relying on others you lose your sense of discerning for yourself. Your guides and angels will communicate whatever messages and meanings anyway they can, and this can be through signs and symbols in the physical world, and it can also be done through your dreams. So please play close attention to your dreams in case they hold messages from your guides and angels. Also do not think that all your messages from your guides and angels are going to be sunshine and roses, or rainbows and butterflies, because at times they will point out that you still may be living in the past or that you have to let something go. However, if the being or entity that is coming through is extremely mean or disrespectful, or gets angry when you ask questions then know that this is not a guide. This would be an astral entity and they may tell you everything you want to hear or others may tell you that you are the worst person ever. As I had already stated in the section 2 preface there's no need to fear at all, because the moment you start feeling that this being may not be of your highest and best good, then that is when you call in Archangel Michael. Then the next step is to ask for Archangel Zadikiel and ascended Masters St. Germaine to calm and purify you with the divine Violet flame.

I would like to tell you a quick story about a friend of mine Debbie. Debbie was trying to connect with her guides and angels and she really wasn't getting anywhere until one day she began to channel. She started to get very interesting information that she had always wanted. This entity was giving her such great answers but then as she started to connect more and more with this being; it became mean, angry, and disrespectful. She then asked it more questions. She began to question where it was from and how was it getting information. She started to think that this was not a guide or an Angel but in fact, an astral entity, who was giving her good information sometimes, but other times it would tell her to hurt her children. It would be mean to her and it would tell her that she was not psychic. Debbie started to become very disheartened by this. She wanted this entity to leave her alone. She had tried the Archangel Michael method and she had tried to call in the divine Violet flame but this entity was attached to her at a very deep level and she couldn't understand why. When Debbie and I met I did not know this. I didn't know that she was still battling with this thing. Now it was not as strong or did not have as much influence as it had in the beginning, because she could recognize now when it was talking to her and she would ignore it. It didn't matter how good or accurate the information was she wanted this thing gone and asked if there was anything I could do. Me being very new to this said I would go into meditation and see if there was anything I could do. What I did when I went into meditation was I asked if there was anything I could do to help Debbie. Then this incantation came through. This incantation is something that you can use if you feel as if a negative entity has attached itself to you and you cannot get rid of it. I cannot guarantee that this will be the end all, be all, but I can tell you from my personal experience this incantation banished the entity that was attached to Debbie. The incantation is as follows: I now call forth Secmet Lord of fire hear my call, hear my plea. I ask you now to please help me to clear _____ of this negative entity fold back time and space let it forget me/him/her in this place. I now call forth Isis, mother of us all to use your staff of power to clear _____ of this negative entity through all time and space so now let it be. I now call forth Lilith goddess of the Nile to help in this endeavor please help _____ now peel back time and space send it back to nothing back to its origin its birth of creation. I now invoke the great God RA hear me now and hear my plea please now cut the cords to this negative entity. Burn the ties and shine your light so he/she/me may be free from this fight. I now call forth and invoke a spiritual court of equity presided over by the Akashic lords 3, now clear _____ of this entity cut the ties that bind it to me/her/him/ and it to me/_____ let it be folded back through time and space let it now forget. I now call forth Michael Metatron and Sophiel to cut the cords to this entity to you with a sword of fire and wings of gold and set back through time and space forever forgetting this place. Let it be shown here and now that _____ is protected by the crown I call forth source for its protection just around her/him/me with divine protection and now prime creator he/she that sees and knows all created all hear my call and hear my plea and now disconnect and recycle this entity this spell is done the die is cast let this story and with all is done now be at peace.

This may be very long but I do know that it works and I send you all my love.

Section 1

Your team!!

Your team what an interesting thing to say about your guides and angels, but that is what they are, a team to help you along your journey. Because in doing so it helps them in their journeys as well. Now you may call your team whatever you wish and no your team is not limited to just your guides and angels. You have ascended Masters, star beings, light beings, elementals, ancestors, departed loved ones, fairies and the list goes on. You have a legion of otherworldly helpers at your disposal. All you have to do to get them to come and assist you with anything is to ask for help! So let's go ahead and meet your team. The first is your guardian angels. Everyone has two guardian angels, the beings that have been with you since you first exited the womb. You have this being that loves you unconditionally and will protect you from whatever your soul has not agreed upon to experience. There is your extroverted guardian angel who will whisper to you. Then there is also an introverted guardian Angel and this angel will stand with you always stroking your aura and filling it with love. You also have access to the Archangels.

There are four major archangels. Archangel Michael, whose name means one who is like God. He is the prince of the archangels and the one who helps you to cut energetic cords to people or places. Michael has a blue aura to him and like all the angels he can be with each one of us all the time. The next Angel is Archangel Uriel. He can help you access the Akashic records, which is your personal book of life that holds your past, present, and future lives. Uriel also helps to heal emotions and can be called upon to enter your heart and help with unconditional forgiveness and to release any anger you may be holding onto. He is also in charge of your crown chakra. This is the chakra at the top of your head that we talked about in a previous chapter. This chakra is all about opening up to universal wisdom and he can assist you in that and his aura is Violet/purple.

Rafael is the next Archangel we will be discussing. His name means God who heals. Rafael helps to heal the physical body. You can call on him when traveling, to make sure that your bags get to their proper location. His aura is emerald green. Rafael is associated with the third eye and heart chakras in the way of opening them and also to help heal them. Archangel Gabriel is the next Archangel we will be talking about. His name means messenger of God. You can call on Gabriel to help you speak your truth or to help you activate your clairaudience ability. Since the throat chakra is connected to your ear chakras this is how he also helps you in communication with the spirit world and with people around you. You can also call on him, Michael and Rafael as well when dealing with matters of the heart. Call on Michael for courage, Gabriel for the right words, and Rafael to open your heart. Now there are a myriad of other angels that you can call upon. I will list some of them below, but of course you can always go online to find more. When doing meditation you can always see what Archangel you are currently working with. There is also a wonderful deck of cards by a man named Stuart Pierce. He made the Angels of Atlantis deck as well as the Angel Heart Sigil's deck. Both of these decks have many different angels within them and I would recommend getting them, if you are interested in learning more about the angels and ways to connect with them.

Ariel: Lion of God/gives courage
Raziel: Secrets of God/helps give you wisdom of the esoteric nature
Jophiel: Joy of God/Beautiful thoughts. Brings joy
Medatron: Guardian or protector/ works with ascension
Sandalphon: He is a protector of earth and a master of music and also known as the angel of prayer. He connects to the earth star chakra
Azrael: Angel of Transition/takes souls to the other side.

There are a multitude of different archangels and angels that you can call upon. This is not an exhaustive list by any stretch of the imagination. This is merely a list of the angels that are easiest to get in contact with and find information on.

Now let's move on to your guides. In my experience you have four main guides. Your first guide is your life to death guide. This guide is with you from your birth to your death. Just like your guardian angel, this will most likely be one of the first guides that you meet. If it is not the first guide you meet, then it may be your animal totem guide. I find those to be the easiest to connect with at first, because they are more connected to the earth. That is the first guide that I met, my animal totem. He was a gray wolf but now when I connect with him, since I have ascended in my consciousness, so has he. He now has changed to a white wolf. These totems are showing you what qualities that you are currently embodying so when I was with the gray wolf, I was teaching people how to be the bridge between spirit and the physical. Now that my wolf is white, I am now the bridge between the physical and the nonphysical and still acting as a teacher. Now do not think that your guides will stay with you throughout your whole life, because a majority of the time they will not. They will stay only until you have learned their lessons. Once you have learned their lessons or they have taught you all that they can, then they will leave and you will get a new guide.

You have tons of help from spirit. You can think of it like a really large support group. Essentially you have 33 groups of 33 guides ranging from star beings, to your great grandma and having a very diverse set of talent. Anything you need assistance with you can get guidance on from your guides, but as I have already stated they will not do the work for you. If your guides did the work for you, then you would lose the experience of living your life. So let's say you need help finding something, then you call on your runner guides and they can lead you to where it is now. These guides can also be used for something I think is amazing like getting you parking, reservations, and appointments. You can think of these guides as your personal assistances and all you have to do is ask and say please and thank you. What I like to do is 20 minutes before I leave I ask for what I want. So if I am traveling somewhere I have never been before, I ask to have light traffic or if we are going to go eat at a restaurant, I ask to have front row parking and to be seated immediately.

I'd like to share a quick story with you about my runner guides and some of the times that I've used them and the amazing results that I've gotten. I remember when I first learned about runner guides from Sonia Choquette. I was a little skeptical and I didn't know if they were real. How could guides run ahead of me and get me different things that I may want??? Well let me tell you that they really can and it really does work! It's just a matter of getting in contact with those guides.

Now your runner guides, are guides that are more connected to the earthly plane so they are much better at getting things done here on the physical plane. I remember that I was taking a friend of mine to the New Age store here in Indiana. I was very excited to take her there. She was extremely interested in spirituality and in accelerating her consciousness and awakening to the more subtle realms of this universe, so I wanted to show her how easy and simple it is. We were going to stop for lunch and we were also going to pick up some groceries for her house. I told her I have a group of car guides that are called runners and we are going to use them today. She looked at me puzzled and said okay. So I sat down and I talked to my runner guides. I said runner guides I ask that you please run ahead for us and see that we have light traffic, that we get to have front parking at the restaurant we were going to, as well as to get served immediately, and be seated right away. Upon walking in I also asked them to have a good server who was nice and quick. I then asked my runner guides to help us find bargains on all the things that my friend needed for groceries. Needless to say everything that I asked for we had gotten. We had almost no traffic on the road. We had front parking at the restaurant. We went in and were immediately seated and our waitress was superfast. At lunch my friend was telling me how amazing that was and how connected I must be. I told her it had nothing to do with how connected I was. It just mattered that I trusted and knew that these guides were around me to assist me in any way possible. it was just a matter of asking and believing that these guides would do what I asked. We then went to the grocery store before heading to the New Age store because it was right across the street. We found great bargains on three out of the 13 things she needed, which in my opinion is still amazing. We then went over to the New Age store and had front parking again. we spent at least 2 ½ to 3 hours looking around the store, looking at crystals, looking up what the crystals did, looking at card decks, and so forth. It was such a wonderful day, and still to this day that friend of mine now uses her runner guides all the time as do I. This is just one example of the different guides that you have you also have

- bargain guides which will help you find bargain
- cooking guides which will help you find teachers as well as new recipes and cookbooks

- music guides which will lead you to new places and new styles of music as well as to a teacher if one is needed
- mechanical guides who can help you find the right mechanic for your car or motorcycle or even boat, they can also help you find bargains and tools that you may need
- art guides that can help you find different art supplies, teachers, different forms of art
- Warrior guides
- Joy guides
- prosperity guides
- healer guides
- wisdom guides
- master guides
- muses
- guardian angels
- master teachers
- divine teachers
- divine helpers
- creative guides
- spirit teachers

There are guides for everything and anything that you may have an interest in. It's just a matter of calling on them. Just because I did not label a guide here, doesn't mean that it's not possible to find the kind that you are looking for. So needless to say whatever type of guidance you need, there will be someone to help you.

Higher-Self

Higher-self is a term associated with multiple belief systems, but its basic premise describes an eternal, omnipotent, conscious, and intelligent being, who is one's real self. Blavatsky formally defined the higher-self as the inseparable ray of the Universe and oneself. The higher-self is your greatest ally on your spiritual journey. The higher-self is you but at a higher dimensional frequency. How I like to describe the higher-self is, the higher-self is on a mountain and you are in a valley and there is fog in the valley. But you and your higher-self have walkie-talkies and your higher-self is able to see where you cannot, it sees the bigger picture. You can connect to the higher-self just like any other guide. The only thing that is different about the higher-self, is that it is connected to your monad or your God head. It is the part of you that is most connected to the divine source. This does take a little bit more practice to do, to get in touch with this higher-self because it's different than your typical guide even though it is a part of you. Like your guides are it's on a higher dimension then you.

CHAPTER 12

See the Signs

This is one of my favorite topics in the intuitive field because there are so many diverse and different ways in which our guides can communicate with us. What I'm going to encourage you to do is to not take my meanings of a symbol, but to come up with your own unique meanings to what the symbols and signs mean to you. How many times have you seen a repetitive number, word or animal? It just seems to be everywhere you look.

I want you to know that you can always ask for signs. I always ask for my signs in the physical and let it be something I understand, however sometimes you may be unaware of something and your guides will try to get your attention through signs and symbols. You may be asking yourself what happens if I don't catch a sign. Believe you me, that isn't a problem for your guides. They will also continuously send you the same sign over and over again until you get it. They will send it in a myriad of different ways because that is how dedicated your guides are to you. I've already told you the story of how I met my guardian angel and the sign I received from him. But let me tell you another story that happened to me when I was opening up to spirit.

It was in the summer of 2013. I was really opening up to spirit a lot more, getting a lot of different intuitive messages from my guides and angels. I was also doing readings for people, and paid readings which were scary. Then at work I started to notice the color purple. We were using a lot of purple at work, purple paper, purple paint, purple crayons, just a lot of purple. At first I didn't think anything of it, until I went home and I started to see a lot of purple at home too. My sister got a new purple outfit. We bought a pack of pens that was supposed to be red but it ended up being purple. On my walks I was noticing people had planted a lot of purple flowers. I still really thought nothing of it. I thought it was just a coincidence and by the way when you start working with spirit you will know that there is no such thing as coincidence only inevitability. So I kept on walking and as I did what I began to notice is more and more purple. The next day when I went to work I noticed more and more of the girls were wearing purple, but purple is a girl color so again I didn't think anything of it. Once again when I went home and went for my walk I actually saw a lady planting purple flowers and I kept being shown purple. Over the next three weeks, purple was everywhere. It didn't matter where I went, what I did, or who I was with, purple showed up everywhere. I even remember one day at work none of the girls were wearing purple, so I thought oh okay it's over now, until one of the dads walked in and he was wearing a purple shirt. All I could do was laugh so later on I went online to try to figure out what the color purple meant.

I found many different meanings but it didn't seem to matter, because purple kept showing up all over the place, so finally I decided that I would go get a reading and see what information I could get. When I went into the room the reader asked me if I had any specific questions, I told him yes. I would like to know why am seeing the color purple everywhere and as I looked down what did he have but a purple amethyst crystal. I busted out laughing and so did the psychic he said, "It looks like you've come to the right place," I said "I guess I have." So the psychic tuned in and when he did, he told me that my guides were trying to show me that I was entering a new level of intuition. I had basically graduated from level I and shot up to level V in a very short amount of time. That was actually my request to my guides to constantly show me that I was actually becoming more intuitive. So they were giving me the signs, it's just that I didn't understand. After I found that information out, the color purple within two days faded away and I didn't see it as much anymore. Then I began to think, how I want the universe /my guides and angels to communicate with me.

I came up with this intention or request to the universe, I asked that the universe treat me gingerly, softly, gently and to give me signs in the physical world that I will understand, and to keep on giving me the message in increasing ways until I get it. And the universe has done just that. It never makes my life fall apart it always gives me gentle messages.

However you can get signs in a myriad of different ways, you can even set up a system with your guides to say that certain objects or visuals mean certain things. Personally for me when I see caution tape that means for me that there is danger and I need to be on alert. This actually works and saved me. I was out with a bunch of friends and we were having a great time. The friend who was supposed to drive me home was drinking a lot but she said she was fine. All of a sudden she said, "Okay it's time to go," so we both stood up but as I did I was drawn to look at the stage where the band was playing. The guitarist was putting on his harness to carry around his guitar and guess what I had seen. Yes, it was caution tape. So I told my friend that we needed to stay just a bit longer because I was going to get us a ride home. So I called a friend of ours and she took us both home. Thank goodness she did, because as soon as we left the bar the police had pulled up and they were actually doing breathalyzer tests. So if we would've left earlier, she and I would've most likely had been arrested and put in jail. That is just one example of how you and your guides can begin to work together to facilitate a life that is guided, easy, magical and amazing. The real key in interpreting signs and symbols is what they mean to you not what they mean to other people. Yes I've gotten help but I do not rely on that help. I rely on what my intuition says and I encourage you to do the same thing. If you want to look things up to get a better understanding that's totally fine, but see what the sign means to you first before going to go look on the Internet.

Final thoughts

I want to thank you so much for reading my book, I hope that it has brought you some clarity and helped you on your intuitive journey. My intention for this book is that it helped to awaken, inspire, and help all those on an intuitive journey, which is nothing more than a journey deeper into self. I want to express to you from an intuitive standpoint from my personal view that I believe being an intuitive is something that everyone has within them. Some people are just awake when they come in, but it that does not mean that you cannot awaken to that level. The more people that awakens to their intuition and uses it, the easier it is for everyone else to do the same. Once you start working with spirit, your guides, your angels and your higher self, you are going to begin to notice something. Your life will start to change. It may be little changes at first, but then it becomes more and more. You will begin to see how easy your life is once you are tuned in to spirit and you are able to tune into your intuition. Life becomes effortless and easy as you tune in and listen.

Printed in the United States
By Bookmasters